Backroads and Barefoot

Mary Green

Mary Green   First edition 2014

Back Roads and Barefoot

Copyright 2014 by Mary Green

All rights reserved. No part of this book may be used or reproduced in any manner whatsoever without written permission of the author except in the case of brief quotations embodied in critical articles or reviews

Scripture quotations, unless otherwise indicated are taken from the King James translation, public domain.

Cover Art by Marie Buchert

Interior Art by Selena Nix

ISBN 978-1-312-61986-9

Acknowledgements

I want to say thank you to all my friends and family for sticking by me through this process of publication. Long hours and lots of tears went in to make this possible. I know it would not be possible if it wasn't for God's guidance and grace. I thank Him so much for sending such a godly group of friends my way. Also a huge thank you to my youth group they have helped me grow in God and challenged me to reach for higher goals. I love each of you very much. My pastor, friend, and mother thank you for all the hours you put in to helping edit and keep me encouraged. For all the years of praying and all you have done for me. My church family for all their support and prayers along the way, of this journey God has taken me on.

Forward

I've had the privilege to watch this young troubled little girl grow into a beautiful godly lady. I would encourage anyone that is going through difficulty or that feels bound by the clutches of darkness to embrace this book and see how the love of Jesus can set you free. The bondage that seems to engulf you may be different of that of the authors; however, He will give you His beauty for your ashes. This book is full of encouragement to keep putting your faith and trust in God and will help you to realize that God can turn anyone around and use them to carry His Gospel.

In service for the King,
Pastor Sonya Nix

Introduction

Pulling out an old picture box full of memories of my childhood, I was forced to ask myself a question. Do you realize how far Jesus has brought you? I closed my eyes while memories of growing up flooded my mind. I didn't grow up in a Christian home, but I did know of the name Jesus; however, I didn't know much more than the name. Jesus, He knew me though, and through all the many roads I traveled he was right there with me, even when I didn't realize it.

I grew up in what seemed a "normal", average family, and I remember spending every weekend on some family owned property deep in the woods. We spent our time together with aunts, uncles, moms, dads, grandparents, and cousins; let's just say the whole family. We spent most of our time swimming in the creek or riding four wheelers. Oh how we enjoyed the company of the entire family every weekend.

While going through pictures of those "normal" years, I was reminded of my 1st grade year in school. I made home coming basketball princess, this was a huge honor. Not only was it a chance to dress up, I got to stand on court with the whole basketball team. There were many fond memories in that old picture box, memories I want my children to have, and ones that put a smile on their face, that bring them to a time of happiness in their life. The pictures in my old picture box stopped around the age of ten and that is where life changed for me.

Life takes its first turn

When I was ten, I found out life wasn't as it appeared. I soon learned my "Dad" was not the man who fathered me. It was then, that life took a turn for the worst, I felt as if I no longer belong in the life I had been living. Not only would things become different in our home, but my storm was just starting. I was soon introduced to the man who was my biological father. As the twist of fate would have it, I also had a brother who was a few years older. Getting to know this new part of my family was strange to say the least. I was unsure what to call these two men or how to act. Should I call him dad? Why am I just learning about this? What about all these people who I thought were my family I remember the confusion this brought; nothing really made since. I wouldn't know until years down the road that this news didn't change who my step-dad was to me.

I struggled to know who I was because my identity seemed to be taken with this news; everything about me began to fade away. What did all those memories with what I thought was my biological family mean? Were they all lies? My life past, present, and future now seemed pointless and the way I thought about people changed. The way I carried myself changed. The sweet kid I had always been was changing. I would find myself looking in the mirror wondering who I was, nothing made sense anymore. On the inside I had spent the last year changing, but I wasn't treated different and I looked the same. I just felt so different; my heart had grown cold and black at such a young age. I felt alone and discarded like curbside trash. Not because I was treated different but because I allowed a piece of information define who I was. The one thing I had always known was no longer real, it was a lie. My whole life was just a faint memory of lies.

I found myself spending a lot of time alone. I would lose myself in music, books, and in thought. I turned to music that would talk of the same things I was feeling, songs I could relate with; it was almost as if they would speak straight to me. They would talk about being all alone or not knowing where they fit in. I not only understood the words; I was living them. I too would infiltrate my mind with books about witchcraft, and books referring of hatred. I chose to read things like this because of its darkness; it appealed to the side of me that was angry and dark. Maybe in hopes I could find a way to just erase everything that had happened. I don't know what it was about these worldly items that kept me so intrigued.

Not knowing the more I filled my mind with the words Satan had published I would soon be his puppet. They say the highway to hell is wide and filled with many. I'm here to tell you, there are back roads to that highway. I spent many years wandering those back roads finding myself lost and alone during most of my teenage years. Looking back, now I realize I was never really alone. I had a friend who walked with me, Jesus. I can honestly say I am ashamed of the places I took Him. My heart even hurts writing these words to share with all of you.

Backroads

I found myself literally living my life on back roads at the age of thirteen. I started drinking because it was easy to get my hands on. There was always something alcoholic in our house. Smoking cigarettes soon followed, as it too, was easily accessible. Rebellion or an escape from reality no matter the reason, I learned that I could get away with things I shouldn't be doing. No one would ever find out and I could do whatever I wanted. My parents were busy and it seemed I was constantly overlooked. During this time I would not face any form of punishment, rebellion at its finest. My thoughts were, "It doesn't matter what choices I make, who will care anyway?"

All of this rebellion led to sneaking out while everyone else was asleep. At first I didn't go far, I would steal a beer and a cigarette and set outside while everyone was asleep; just to have that time to escape all my own reality. Little did I know, as I sat alone on my steps in the middle of the night I would soon be on a different back road. Yes, there are many back roads to hell. We may not see that the little path we are on leads to a highway of destruction and misery; but it does. Those small paths in the middle of nowhere lead to some nasty places. These places turn you into someone you never wanted to be; places that break you down so low that it seems as if there is no hope left for you and it took me years to realize it.

My late nights outside alone soon became late nights outside with guys. At first it was nothing more than someone to talk with. At the time, that void I felt from my biological dad being absent and the man I thought was my dad not being real was filled by these guys. They took time to come down to where I was and hang out. Filling that empty feeling I had with words; that at the time seemed like so much more. It seemed so easy for them to complement me. I couldn't imagine why someone would tell me how cool I was or that I was pretty. I felt so empty and black, they made me feel safe and secure with them. Little did I know, as I felt comfortable having them around, their motive was not to help me; their motive was to break me down even more. I would soon become a victim of kind words and good looks.

At first things seemed to go so slow it took a few years of me fading away to get to those nights on my steps. However, once I was on those steps, my wandering on back roads went deeper into the darkness and fast. I realize now that choices matter so much, what may not seem bad to you at the time can quickly send you spiraling out of control. I'll never forget one night in particular, as I think about it tears stream down my face. This night sent me deeper into my darkness and shattered every last piece of feeling like a person I had, the last emotional possession that remained mine the last time I would feel more than just a broken being.

Thinking of this night not only saddens me, I relive that fear like it was yesterday, like no time has gone by. Only one of those guys showed up. He didn't come to offer kind words or complements instead he offered his touch. Something I had never had before, I was so scared, yet didn't want to appear weak. Now I know that I was weak by not standing up for myself, for not getting myself out of that spot. I let this person do whatever he wanted and I didn't fight back, I'm not sure I knew how. What seemed like hours lasted only a few short minutes and he disappeared, nothing special about it at all; I felt so disgusting, used, and dirty. What most people plan their whole life for waiting on that special person, time, and place so that it is a lasting memory of something special, was the most disgusting thing I had experienced this far in my life. Not only was there nothing special, but I had no voice in the matter, I was a place for him to come and take whatever made "him" feel better. Just an object for his taking, surely, it was my fault? I let this happen? I made myself available to become his victim at his disposal? I spent days tossing all these questions around, blaming myself for being so stupid for allowing this to happen, I felt as though it was my fault. I never said anything for fear I would be the one in trouble for allowing this to happen, for making myself available to this tragedy. I let this man, my victimizer, get away with no consequences, with no punishment because I felt as though I got what I deserved for doing the things I had been doing. Instead, I would take this as my own punishment I was paying for my own mistakes, I felt I deserved this.

Speak up

Looking back I realize how foolish I was to think such a thought. No matter what choices you are making you do not have to be a victim with no voice. My prayer would be that no female or male would ever have to go through a situation like this. In reality I know this happens more often than not, if you have found yourself in this spot or even someone you know is in this spot, Speak up! That fear you have shouldn't keep you quite, your voice may save another person or yourself from having to go through any form of sexual assault. If you don't already talk to the Lord, start and let him guide your steps not only will it take courage to speak up but the situation will take strength. Ask the Lord to also do a healing weather the victim is you or someone you know.

The Lord can begin to heal you or them. No one can give you back what a person like that takes; however, you don't have to live in that moment ever again. You can get back your life with the help of the Lord. He can make you a new person, one who doesn't live in fear, doubt, or pain. He can make you whole again.

It's up to you to decide to let God mend your brokenness, but if you decide to let Him, not only will life be "ok" again it can be so much better than what it ever was. I encourage everyone to pray for those who have had to face this kind of abuse, that the Lord would heal, strength, and pick up the broken ones. Ask the Lord do what only He can do, for Him to send in armies of angels to protect and guard those in need. That He would give strength and courage to those who need to speak up, that he give peace like only He can give to.

Talk spreads fast

I felt I had to keep this night a secret; it was my fault, right? Little did I know that this man left me to go brag to every one of his friends and collect on a bet that was made for who could sleep with me first. Not only was I fighting the disgusting feeling and the quilt I felt for not stopping this guy, but now I had to fight the reputation I had just been given for letting this man do the things he did and for what he had taken from me. Overnight I was given a reputation of easy. I didn't go looking for this reputation it came looking for me. I see now that we have got to be careful of every step we take. I had only taken two steps out of my front door. Those two steps lead me in a place I never intended to go and very quickly. Satan is roaming to and fro seeking whom he may devour, that night he devoured me and I didn't even realize what had happened. It left me thinking I was stuck with this title this man had given me. I became a victim to a name tag that was placed on me.

Every time I walked out my door I could hear people whispering and laughing as they called me a whore, easy, or just mock me. It took everything I had to keep walking past these people without telling them I wasn't either of those things and that the only reason he could say he "slept" with me was because he took it. I decided after weeks of hearing people's talk that was not true. Maybe it would be easier to live up to the name tag. If people already thought I was easy then why not just become what they were saying. I would sleep with people and become what they were saying. At first it was to make truth of the lies and at this point I thought this course of action gained back what was ripped away from me that night. Thinking if I was the one putting myself out there instead of someone just taking what they wanted I would gain back what was stolen this way I could be in control of my life and not someone controlling me. I was wrong again! I wished I had known then what I know today. Jesus was more than a name, He wanted to jump in and help me, He loved me and was just waiting on me to come to Him; He would have made me new again. If I had known this maybe I wouldn't have tried to fix things myself because I was making a huge mess of this life He had given me. He didn't have these plans for me he had good plans and I was taking one wrong turn after another.

I never said a word to my parents or anyone else, but talk spreads fast. A few months down the road my mom never said a word but had made an appointment for me to get on birth control. When I found out I thought I was never going to be able to leave my house again. Part of me wished that would happen so I could never be taken advantage of again. We went in for the doctor's appointment to find out birth control was out of the question. I was thirteen and pregnant; I was overwhelmed by a mighty rush of darkness. I felt so angry and confused how could this happen? 'Are you serious?" I thought to myself. I'm a walking disaster, it felt like my chest would cave. I couldn't breathe, I looked over at my mother expecting to see anger or disappointment, there was no emotion as if she didn't hear what the nurse said. The nurse sent us home with tons of pamphlets on abortion, adoption, and kids with kids. At that moment, just that quick, in the doctor's office my family knew what I had been doing. To my surprise my family never punished me for my sexual lifestyle; however, a baby seemed to be the real issue for them.

My life would never be the same; I was going to have a baby, but wait I'm a kid myself. I didn't know what it meant to take care of someone, I couldn't even take care of myself! What was I going to do? My family began making decisions for me. Abortion would be what my family thought was the best choice; just kill the baby and forget this ever happen and we could all go back to "normal". I read all the pamphlets over and over knowing that I would have to make a choice soon, but how can I make this huge decision at such a young age? I didn't want to raise a baby, but I didn't want to kill one either. Could I really give it away? I know what it feels like to find out your family isn't biological. Would I want someone feeling the way I felt? What do I do? How do I escape this? I honestly didn't know what to do. I couldn't make this decision; I tossed everything around for the next few weeks.

Time for my checkup came quickly and I would have to talk with the nurse about what I would do. I knew what my family wanted me to do and being so young I didn't know if I would have a say in the matter at all. I remember waiting in the cold room alone for what seemed like hours for this nurse to come in the room. The nurse told me that my test had come back and I had miscarried; there was no decision to make my body had aborted the baby. Tears streamed down my face, as much as I hate saying this it was a mix of emotions joy, relieve, and sadness; I have never felt so many emotions at once. With no hesitation and the absence of sensitivity the nurse quickly moved to the next issue at hand, safe sex, she took no time telling me how to prevent this from happening again.

Where was the love?

Again I was sent home with pamphlets to read I spent the next few weeks thinking about all that just happened. How my whole life was almost changed forever at thirteen. I thought about how lucky I was; yet, I was torn with sadness that I had lost someone who might have truly loved me. You would think this would be a breaking point for me, that it would have woke me up a little. Maybe now I would decide to try turning my life around for the good? Now being a parent myself I can't help thinking why my mother wouldn't have set me down and talked to me and showed me how to act. She didn't do any such thing, the whole situation was "swept under the rug" like it never even happened. No one in the family ever talked about it again, I dealt with all the emotions on my own. Why not lock me up? Sure I would have been mad, I was a teenager thinking I was all grown. As a parent today, I want to do all I can to protect my kids. I will never understand why this was never talked about again in my family? Why my Mother never tried to be a mom? Why my pregnancy was just put in a box and locked? Around this time I began to feel a lot of hatred for my mother. I may have been young and wild but I still longed for love and direction but no one seemed to give it to me. I was left to just run wild and destroy my own life, no one seemed to care at all about any choices I made.

It was here where I found myself changing courses on the back roads. I was given no consequences for my actions, no baby, and no parental lock up I was free to go back living the same life I had been living. It seemed as if no one cared that I was throwing my life away. All I wanted was for someone anyone at this point to reach out and love me. I felt completely dead inside no emotions remained. I don't know if you have ever been truly emotionless? This is a place that is so dark and cold. Even your own life becomes unimportant, and seems completely meaningless. Feelings of, no one really would miss me or no one would care if they walked in and found me dead on my bed one morning began to flood my mind. I'm not sure I can really express how painful this place is, similar to someone turning lights off on life. The world is no longer in color everything is now black and white. I would look at someone who was happy and it made me want to scream! It's like watching someone die to only realize you're watching yourself die a slow death.

Then there was blood.

This led to a new addiction, one that would become a daily activity. I became a cutter not for sympathy; I just longed to feel again. I had no tears left, no real emotions so I started taking a blade and cutting down my arms not caring if I cut to deep. Even when I was cutting I felt very little pain. The sight of blood pouring from my arms was the only thing that brought a bit of emotion to me. I knew only living things bled. All I needed was a moment to know I was still living.

Leviticus 17: 13) "Whatever man of the children of Israel, or of the strangers who dwell among you, who hunts and catches any animal or bird that may be eaten, he shall pour out its blood and cover it with dust; 14) for it is the life of all flesh. Its blood sustains its life. Therefore I said to the children of Israel, 'You shall not eat the blood of any flesh, for the life of all flesh is its blood. Whoever eats it shall be cut off.'

I didn't know at the time about the many verses on blood and the importance it holds. I want to point out in this particular passage where it states, "Blood sustains its life." During this time I knew nothing about these verses nor would I have understood the meaning. God was dealing with me during this time; however, I didn't feel him working nor did I realize it. Since seeing my blood is what gave me a bit of emotion; even then the blood was sustaining me. I don't encourage anyone to ever cut themselves. I simply want to share my experiences blood is what sustains life and without it there is only death. I could have very easily cut to deep or the wrong way and took my own life, sent myself to spend an eternity in hell, but at the time I didn't care. Today I know hell is not where I want to spend my eternity and I'm thankful for another chance.

We can also find in the bible the story of the man in Gadarenes. He stayed alone wandering the mountains, crying, and cutting his self with pieces of stone. Cutting isn't a new issue in fact it has been around long before any of us, a real issue that affects a lot of people. You're not only left with scars that don't go away on your physical body; you are left with memories of the things which lead you to cut in the first place. The memories that will try to define you for the rest of your life every time you see the scars you will be reminded of what was occurring during that time in life. Satan will use those scars as a constant reminder of who you once were making you think you will be nothing more than "that" cutter. Jesus, He came and freely gave His life so that you wouldn't have to be defined by your mistakes, so you can be made new again. He made a choice to love you more than His own life so you could make a choice to follow Him and teach others of His love.

Mark 5: 1) And they came over unto the other side of the sea, into the country of the Gadarenes. 2) And when he was come out of the ship, immediately there met him out of the tombs a man with an unclean spirit, 3) Who had his dwelling among the tombs; and no man could bind him, no, not with chains: 4) Because that he had been often bound with fetters and chains, and the chains had been plucked asunder by him, and the fetters broken in pieces: neither could any man tame him. 5) And always, night and day, he was in the mountains, and in the tombs, crying, and cutting himself with stones.

What happens next is this man ran to Jesus when he seen him walking his way Jesus was able to rid this man of his possession of demons. Now I'm not saying all cutters are possessed with demons I will say though that there is an inner issue a spirit of depression, anger, or hatred I can't tell you your story. Only you and Jesus know your story and I encourage you to talk to Jesus as He can free you of that spirit that may have a hold on your life. Just like the man Jesus freed in this story even though this man was freed of the demons the people in town did not want this man to stay around they told him to leave and not come back. Jesus told this man to go home to his family his friends and to tell them all of what works was done. He wanted him to share his testimony to tell of the good works that Jesus had done for him.

Why share your testimony?

If you have overcome cutting or any other battle, share what Jesus has done. Your story may just help someone else. Jesus deserves the glory for all the good works He does. If sharing what He has done for you helps someone, wouldn't you want to do that?

I wouldn't want cutting to be a resource for anyone I will encourage those who cut and even those who know people who cut to talk to Jesus and seek wise council. How do I do that you may be saying; I tell people all the time there is no special way to talk to Jesus I talk to him just like I do you. It may be as simple as "Hey Jesus, I need you!" Sometimes we can't get the words to come out but the great thing about Jesus is he knows what you're saying even when you can't speak. It's easy to call out the things we want or need to the Lord, but we must remember to thank Him. So many times I remember either yelling at Him or rambling off my list of request without ever thanking Him. Thank Him for the things He does the blessings He gives you. He deserves so much more than just demands from us.

During the time I was cutting I would finally see some consequence for my actions not what I wanted, but at least someone finally took a stand. My "Step-Dad" had decided that it was time for me to get checked into a rehab. I was shipped off to a mental hospital for evaluation. Now at this time in my life I had become really good at closing up and dealing with issues myself. I knew how to put on a good act. When I arrived at the hospital I was stripped of everything I had; everything that posed a threat to my life or anyone else's in there, even my shoe laces. I don't remember every detail of what happened while in rehab, but I do remember some of the girls saying they had been there for months. I knew I could not spend months in that place; I had to get out and quick. So I followed all the rules, turned on the kindness element, and played like a good girl. I would tell the therapist what I thought they wanted to hear and within the week. It was determined that I was fine and just had an off day. I knew this wasn't the case, but by no means did I want to stay in this place any longer than I had to. I would put on a smile through the day and spend most of the night crying in my bed in hopes this place would soon be just a memory I could forget. I spent two weeks total in this place waiting for everything to be finalized so I could go home. That ride home, no one spoke, we just simply rode in the car with pure silence. After getting home I spent a lot of time alone in my room thinking over the last few weeks to realize I still didn't really find what I was looking for. Someone did step up and show a little effort but it was mainly ditching me in someone else's lap, "the rehab".

I was determined to find love at this point in any way I could. I didn't care what, where, or why I made the choices I thought I had to make. In desperation to fill this void, I looked for "love" where ever I could. I continued to search for it in every man I could. I would fill that emptiness I felt by just laying down with whomever. Approximately by the age of fifteen I had added methamphetamines to my list of things that I could fulfill that emptiness with. It was easy to get invited to any party or just out for the night when you were willing to get high and sleep around, it was as if everyone else was also on a quest to wreck their life and didn't even know it. (As a female I learned quickly that I could use my body to gain whatever I wanted, in that moment it might be drugs, or a drink, or even someone to just kill a few hours with so I wouldn't have to face my own reality.) There were lots of times I would sleep with people expecting to feel nothing, just to be able to simply run away from reality in that moment. There were also times I thought by giving all I had would allow someone to really want me for me not realizing that there was nothing else for anyone to want when I was so freely giving everything away. The next few years nothing would change; I would keep living this "out of control" life style in hopes of something I would not find.

Was it real?

There was one person during this time in my life who I could open up my heart to, I could tell him anything and most of the time I did. He would let me just talk or yell if that is what I needed, I remember thinking how odd it was to be able to really tell someone what I was feeling. Not only did this person hear me but it was as if they really understood me like he related to the pain and emptiness I felt. We would both talk about getting away from this small town as if this town was the only reason we lived the way we lived. I remember spending many of the nights in his truck in the middle of the woods just talking and laying under the stars in hopes we would find the answer to all our problems out there in the middle of nowhere. It took very little time until I would find myself thinking about this person all the time, I would get lost in thoughts about him and I running away together to find a better life out there somewhere. Every girls dream is to find that one person who you could truly be yourself around. I longed for any and every moment I would see this young man; there was just something about him that made me forget even if for a short time of all the stuff that had happened in my life. I would offer all I had to this man, my heart, soul, and body. He knew me better than anyone maybe even better than I knew myself. He too was searching for something because he was just as lost as I was. His life style was a mirrored image of mine his actions were the same as my actions.

The fairy tale was no "happily ever after," no girl meets boy falls in love and runs away to live this wonderful life together. We both would find ourselves lost in drugs and sex trying to fill that black hole we both had. As much as I cared for this person that selfish part of me was still out to destroy and he ended up in the crossfire. We never dated just remained friends he understood what I was doing because he was doing the same thing. I was so wrapped up in my path of destruction that we knew taking that chance on each other would have ruined the only real friendship either of us had. It was painful and hard to realize that the one person you can tell everything to you could never be with. You can't share a life together because you would end up destroying one another.

Not being able to have the one person I wanted and it being no one's fault but mine left me treating people the way I would not want to be treated. I was short and cold with people, no real emotion, and never getting attached to anyone. I built walls that no one would be able to break down; I did not want to let anyone in. If I could not be with whom or be what I wanted then I wanted nothing at all and I did not want anyone else to have anything either. I just wanted to cause people the same pain I felt; loneliness, worthless, and unlovable at this point in my life. I would find that not even sex, drugs, or drinking would fill this void anymore I would find myself searching for a new way to fill this void I had.

Then there was Church

Let's jump back a few years somewhere in the time frame of thirteen I can't remember the exact date nor all the details, but I do remember that one of my cousins on my step dad's side took me to church, a small Pentecostal Church. That first day was an experience to never forget to say the least. The Youth pastor was loud, strange, and had this red hair that matched this huge birth mark on her face. I remember thinking that there must have been some real issues with her no way was she your "average" person. No one could be this crazy and still be considered sane. She would try to get me to get involved in her class by asking me questions about the Bible. I would always answer any question with "ditto" I didn't know the answers to her questions and I wasn't sure I really wanted to know them. After her class ended there would be the main church service which was loud; music, people flopping around, jumping over things, and talking in some weird language. I remember thinking "What in the world have I walked into?" Even as weird as it appeared, I found it to be intriguing. I watched all the moves being made. I became eager to know why they were doing such things and yet couldn't imagine myself ever acting in such a manner! I would return to the little church a few times as my curiosity had the best of me. The Youth Pastor would constantly try to get me to be involved my answer remained the same unless it was a trip or an event that seemed fun then I would be there. As for class and learning what the bible had to say I tried to stay as far from learning as possible. Expect for the parts I felt could be used for my benefit. Let me remind you during this time I continued the wild life style I was living. I had enough guilt going on I didn't want anything else to make me feel bad or require me to question my actions.

My heart was dark and cold and my outward appearance tended to reflect that as I would dress as dark as I could, one might say "gothic" attire. I would listen to every word said at the church I often found myself even reading along with them observing every action. I heard what they were saying but I never really understood so one day I decided to ask a question. "How do you know some strange dude like thousands of years ago didn't just write the bible and make all this up so people would follow his rule book?" The youth leader replied "I don't know, but I would rather die and it not be real then die and it be real and burn in hell." I will never forget those words and as a youth pastor myself today, I'm sure I have used this saying more than once. Today I write this as a youth pastor in the same Pentecostal Church. It may have taken a long time getting where I am today, but I know God was in control of every move.

I heard what she said and for the first time I understood why they did what they did. Faith drove them to read, study, and live out the words of the bible because they had faith! I believed I was too far gone and lost on the back roads for their God to want anything to do with me. I remained in the church for some time while continuing to live the life I had been. I began to realize the emptiness I was trying to fill was getting filled on Sundays and Wednesdays. I found kneeling beside the church alters and crying would help at the moment. After kneeling at that old time alter, my reality called "life" remained still hurt, scared, and confused and I couldn't understand why my life seemed to be such a disaster. One of the first conversations with God was about how unfair my life was. I did not understand why the Creator of man whom he loved so much would put me in such a bad place. That first talk with God was pure anger, I screamed and blamed God for everything. Soon I would find my anger began to turn to remorse, I started feeling bad for my action's and I knew I was the one to blame not God, after all, I was the one making choices that were bad. Instead of turning my life around I found it easier to run from God and not wanting to change my life style. Instead of finding my rescue in Jesus and changing my ways, I decided that I could manage life alone. I didn't need God or anything that came with church and I thought I would be fine on my own.

It seemed that every time God revealed an answer to my problems I would run from it and sink myself a little deeper in the hole of self-pity. What I didn't realize during this time is that my selfishness not only was hurting me but in reality hurting everyone around me. I used people for what I could gain. At the moment I may not have seen it that way, I thought I was the only one with something to really lose. How many times has God sent us the answer and we have just ran as far away from it as possible?

Black magic

I want to touch base on an issue that was very much real for me. I mentioned that I had spent a lot of time reading on black magic and how it works. Not only was I drinking, doing drugs, sleeping around, and cutting myself I practiced black magic. I was reading tarot cards, playing ouija boards, and preforming séance's. I myself would never believe this stuff was real if I hadn't watched it happen with my own eyes. I can only try to bring to life the way these things made me feel it was like a taking over of my mind and body. I remember reading about similar stories in the Bible where the enemy would take over and people would be possessed by the force of hell that drove them. I was able to see things that not everyone could see and I would even hear things that no one else could hear. As I continued on this path I grew darker almost as if I was trapped inside a black box, like I was a vapor in this whole other being. Those dark spirits had attached themselves to me and would control my actions; I had become their puppet on a string. There were many of times I would pass out here or there from being up for days due to my drug usage. Never worrying something would happen to me during this time because I felt protected as long as I wasn't fighting these spirits, as if, they were making sure I was ok. I would wake up to other people telling me that when they would get close to me they could see these dark silhouettes of people all around me, people seemed really scared of what they witnessed. Thinking they were crazy until one day I was walking past a glass window and caught my reflection and I was not alone I saw what they had all seen, I could never make out a face but I seen huge silhouettes in dark capes all around me. Honestly it scared me and as long as I couldn't see it I was fine but when I seen this army of black following me I was scared I had no idea how to stop what was happening. I didn't run back to church but I did start reading my Grandma's old bible; however, the more I read the more these forces attacked me as if I would never break free; like I had sold my soul to the devil and I was stuck in this forever.

There are a few other types of experiences I want to share with you, for instance, we would go out late of a night to ghost hunt at cemeteries way out in the woods and we would sit and watch for odd or paranormal activities. One night we were on our way to a little cemetery way out in the middle of nowhere down a long old dirt road. On the way there that night I can remember seeing a black cow in the middle of the road we had to swerve to get around it and shortly down the road this hound dog was standing in the middle of the road starring right at me with this look of death in his eyes it was as if he was looking directly in my soul. We slammed on the brakes and the dog turned and

666 was branded on his side just as quick as it appeared the dog was gone disappearing deep in the woods; this erry feeling came over me as we continued down the road almost like something was screaming turn around. I didn't know what to do and never said a word. Overcome by this fear that gripped me, I stayed planted in the truck after arriving to the cemetery as if the thin body of the truck would protect me from whatever was out there. Looking across the cemetery I begin seeing all these different figures walking around and they would look at me almost as if they were calling for me; I feared for the worse. I knew the people I came with that were outside the truck was not safe but, I didn't know what to do. I honked the horn on the truck and begged to just go, I didn't want to say what I seen, I just wanted to get out of there. Everyone loaded up and we were pulling out. As we left I could hear these high pitched screams not like screams of help but screams of fear and pain; we could not get out of there fast enough. Back on that dirt road that night as we drove away from the cemetery there were groups of animals: I remember 100's of animal's: rabbits, squirrel, birds, dogs, and opossum and we would have to slam on our brakes many of times. I thought we would never make it off that road in one piece; it seemed that those black figures were out to kill us that night. After we arrived back home I was getting out of the truck and walked around to the back of the truck to see marks that looked like

someone or something had ran their fingers along the dust of the truck. These marks did not match up to the width that any of us could spread our fingers to. I don't know if something really made these marks but I have seen enough in my life to know that anything is possible; this night I thought would be my last.

Matthew 8:28 28) And when he was come to the other side into the country of the Gergesenes, there met him two possessed with devils, coming out of the tombs, exceeding fierce, so that no man might pass by that way. 29) And, behold, they cried out, saying, What have we to do with thee, Jesus, thou Son of God? art thou come hither to torment us before the time? 30) And there was a good way off from them an herd of many swine feeding. 31) So the devils besought him, saying, If thou cast us out, suffer us to go away into the herd of swine.32) And he said unto them, Go. And when they were come out, they went into the herd of swine: and, behold, the whole herd of swine ran violently down a steep place into the sea, and perished in the waters.

My favorite part of this passage is that even the demons had to ask and obey Jesus what a mighty man this has to be that even demons have to listen. That means in the many times I was out "ghost hunting" Jesus was protecting and only allowing what he wanted the whole time. He has a plan even when we have no clue of what it means to have a relationship with him. Of all the times ghost hunting and playing with evil, all the demons and things I seen, He was looking out for me and I didn't know it. With all the brushes from the dark side, I had Jesus protecting me and He had a plan even until this day. I get chills just thinking about some of the things I have experienced. I know that these events really took place and that there is dark and evil spirits roaming around. Satan is trying to get whomever he can and succeeds daily in getting his hands on people. The devil uses all kinds of tactics but the Lord is also working and he is turning what the devil used to harm you into a tool for God's glory. Things like the events that happen to me happen all over every day Christians need to step up their prayer life because there are people who need your prayer and they don't even know it. Start praying for bonds to be broken for those you know and those you don't. I have youth today who ask me if I believe in demons or spirits and I answer yes and tell them about my experience. My experience isn't the only reason I believe. We can find in Matthew 8:28-32 that Jesus cast demons out of two men.

Those demons were commanded to leave. They were cast into a bunch of pigs that then went crazy and ended up falling into sea and drowned; that same power is possible with your prayers.

My road led out of town

There came a time I would find any place other than home to stay, I would stay gone for weeks at a time bouncing from house to house. Until the summer had arrived and I decided to move off with a family friend she was much older than me and I thought that she would be the one who would step up and be what I had been searching for and be that one I could always count on. At first It was amazing, she worked at this little lake side bar and I would go and hang out, even though I was under age, I looked older and back then this wasn't a big issue in small town America.

One night we would find ourselves on the way to a party that she said that a couple of guys had invited us to. Along the drive she introduces me to cocaine for the first time in a truck stop bathroom. She showed me first how to consume it. Cocaine was taken the same as other drugs I had done. She watched the door as I proceeded to get high. The high came quick and instantly I felt amazing like nothing could touch me; unlike other drugs it was smooth quick high. We got back in the car and continued driving until finally we had arrived at the party which happens to be only two guys. I was about to find out that she wanted to get together with the one guy and promised to bring a friend for his roommate, basically, I had just been pimped out by the one person I thought was a real friend. As I was taken back by this news, I was given a few drinks and told that, "if I didn't want to do anything then it would be fine, I didn't have to." Ok, this put my mind at ease and I was free to relax and just drink a little, the night wouldn't go anyway I didn't want it to. Next thing I remember is waking up in a bed with my clothes tossed on the floor tears; begin to roll down my face as I tried to remember what had happen. I didn't know if I could find the strength to come out of the bed, I just wanted to die; I was so embarrassed, ashamed, and angry at my friend. As I stumbled out of the bed, head pounding, I quickly got dressed and walked into the front room; no one was around but a lot of evidence of an extremely wild night. Pill bottles, dirty mirrors, pipes, and empty glasses laid all around. I don't know what all took place that night; I have no memory of anything shortly after drinking. I glanced out the window to see the car I had arrived in, still parked outside, I look around for a bathroom so I could try and clean some of the filthy feeling off of me. I got out of the shower, got dressed, and cleared a spot on the sofa and just sat on full alert, I sat there for what had to been four hours before any movement in the house. My friend came to tell me we would be staying another night. I begged her to just take me home or she could take me to the bus stop, whatever, I just wanted to go. I didn't ask what happened, I didn't want to know, I tried to just forget where I had found myself that morning. She said, "I was acting crazy and that I just needed to relax and all would be fine," that statement angered me and somehow changed me all at once. I said, "ok," she obviously didn't care what had happen or even if I was alright; my only defense came to surface, to hurt back! I pulled myself together, got up, and helped clean up the place. Soon other people would arrive, this time there was around 5 guys who showed up. This night I decided I wouldn't drink and when offered a drink I would secretly pour it out. I did do more cocaine I needed something that would block my mind; I couldn't do what I was about to do sober. I watched and I waited until the man "my friend" came to see stepped in his room for something and I followed him, I would push myself on him in hopes she would catch us. I wanted her to feel the same nasty used feeling I woke up feeling. Well she walked in the room and caught us, she was so mad that she left me there with no ride home; that was not in my plan as foolish as that sounds. I was forced to get a bus ticket and get myself back home, I had one of the guys drop me off at a bus station in the middle of the night with nothing but my purse and just enough cash to get home to my parents. I remember just piling up in my bed for days after getting home, continuously going over what had happened. I knew that what I did was disgusting and I was truly ashamed. I just had no sense of caring about right from wrong. I had no respect for anyone or even myself. I thought over and over that there would never be any hope for me; I was too far gone for any kind of hope at all in my life.

It didn't take long until I was back into my old circle of acquaintances, people had seemed to change while I was gone. Some had even increased their usage of meth to the point they didn't even look the same. Some had gotten off the drugs and had cleaned up, as for me, my reputation had remained the same. Time had changed nothing for me, I was the same cold heartless user that everyone said I was.

At some point, I had thought that maybe my reputation was changing as some people would be so nice until they got what they want. I was so blinded by the fact of what was happening because I was longing for some attention, so desperate that it didn't even matter. I would do anything just to have those five minutes of feeling special, to only be left feeling worse than before. The sad part is, I knew before it even happened what the outcome would be; I just didn't care.

Looking leads to my Father

I wasn't finding that love in any of the things I was choosing. I thought maybe if I would be able to have a relationship with my biological father, then I could find that love, I felt, I was missing. I would go and visit him and I can remember him coming over with my bother and visiting me. I remember this as "a good thing." I can even remember my step dad working on a go-kart for my brother they all seemed to get along. I remember my biological father would always bring me a little money or some crazy item like a snake he had caught. I remember 4th of July being a big deal and He never missed a 4th that he didn't bring fireworks or money to me. I don't remember Christmas or any other holiday being a time I would see my biological dad. Thinking back I was ok with the way our relationship was for a while, it was as if he would come and go, basically paying me off. I guess I thought it was his way of catching up on what he had missed.

Somewhere in the middle of him coming and going I realized that my "step dad" was my dad and would always be. There would still be times I would get mad or feel lost and I would run to this man, my biological father, who I thought should have been in my life. I would mostly found him in the bar as he spent most every waking minute drinking his life away; he was an alcoholic. I had no room to judge; I knew, even if no one else did who and what I was I spent most of my time doing things that I shouldn't be doing also. One day I went to the bar looking for my "escape," I was angry and lost thinking I would find some fulfillment by running to my biological father. I found this man who could barely set on the bar stool without falling over, he must have been there all day drinking. He turned and said, "Look at me no one would ever have to know." He then placed his hand on my chest and he said, "What do you think?" I quickly got up from the stool I was on, never saying a word, and just ran out of the bar. The very person who helped give me life was ready to take advantage of me. I tried to think of every possible reason this had happen, "did I do something to cause this?" I never said a word to anyone. I wouldn't go to see this man again and I would make sure if he came around that someone else would be with me. Often, I would write when I couldn't find any way to get the words out of my mouth and I wrote my biological father a poem I never had the courage to give it to him; I'm not sure I ever would have and as he is no longer walking this earth I won't have the chance to now.

I have let my step-dad read it; as I wanted him to know that even though we may not be blood related, He is very much my Daddy. Just maybe it will be the words you never could say so I will share it with you. If you're struggling with a step parent maybe you will be able to see things differently. Maybe you feel as though life isn't fair and you have been placed in the wrong family, you may even be adopted and feel as though you were abandoned by your biological parents. Whatever your situation, it may be the words you need to read. I will never understand why my father done what he did and I have learned that I don't have to understand circumstances such as these. I have since been able to forgive this man for his actions toward me; it was one of the hardest things. I will never hear I'm sorry from him; but I don't have to relive that for the rest of my life either.

Dear Father

You know I'm your daughter,
Yet never have you been my father.
Your own kid your flesh and blood,
You abandoned me left me to flood
So many places with my lonely tears
Left to have all these different fears,
Many times I just sat and wonder,
But often all I hear is roars of thunder.
Why is it you do not know me?
Is this how it's always going to be?
Thankfully other things I have had,
Like another man I've called Dad!

Someone new

I would finally meet someone new, I was around fifteen at the time, I didn't know then; but, this person would be my help, my changing point. We met while I was out partying I don't remember how but we ended up dating and I decided, "You know maybe this is the change I need," So I talked this man into going to church with me. We walked in that night sat down towards the back. They started as they normally would and somewhere in the middle of the song service the Pastor's wife at that time stood up grabbed a microphone and stated, "Mary, you are headed straight for Hell!" Instantly, I was filled with anger; I don't even know if she said anything after that. I just knew that I was mad and embarrassed. I just could not believe she shouted that in a microphone in front of the whole church and in front of a man whom she didn't know that had never set foot in a Pentecostal Church in his whole life. I didn't leave, I stayed the whole service. I was so mad that I couldn't move or even say anything; no alter for me that night I just sat there. After church we got up and walked out. We climbed in this man's truck and as we were leaving he said, "Do they always tell people they are going to hell?" I was speechless "NO." I had never heard them just call someone out before in all the times I had been there. I knew I wasn't going to make Heaven but I didn't want anyone telling me I was going to Hell either and frankly I didn't think that was the whole churches business. Shortly after I decided to change everything, not because of this woman and if I was to be honest I held a lot of hatred for this woman and I was determined to prove her wrong. Together this man and I made a lifestyle change, but it wasn't easy and we struggled with a few things. We ended up married the summer I turned 16. I thought, wow, I did it I got out of this life I had been lost in for so long. I was listening in church, I was learning, understanding what it was about and was getting involved. I still struggled to really talk about what I was feeling and wanted so bad for people to understand why I had lived the way I did. Even with my life being changed and trying to start a whole new life my past was still taunting me. It was soon after I got married that I wrote my first poem about Christianity and that I realized what I had been looking for was only found in Jesus.

Never Alone

As a little girl I found myself alone without any friends,
Going into my early teen years I watch my life as it ends,
I was alone in a world that scared me,
What would I do who would I be,
I watched other people change before my eyes,
Would these people ever realize,
Who I was what I was about,
I felt as though I wouldn't get out,
Like I was stuck in time,
Everything was just a rhyme,
I soon realized I wanted love,
This I never hand any of,
I slept with guys to feel more,
But instead I was called a whore,
What did this word mean?
I was just a human being,
Then I learned about a word called drugs,
From what I called friends others called thugs,
This thing made me become bold,
In reality it just made me cold,
I began to realize I didn't want to be,
And I didn't think anyone would miss me,
Time and time I attempted suicide,
No one was standing by my side,
Until one day He appeared out of nowhere,
Took my hand and said I'm here,
My child you have work to do,
And I have always loved you!

I wouldn't realize until later on in life what this poem really meant.

Things were great at first at least in our marriage. I had quit school to home school so I could still get my diploma and still fill the roles I needed to as a wife. We both worked full time, we lived in his parent's rent house, and we attended church on a regular basis. Things were good and life was completely different than what it had ever been. I was happy and was able to experience things I had never experienced thus far, I finally knew what it was to truly be cared about. That strange Youth Pastor began to become my friend; we would go and hang out with her and her family, we would play cards, and have couples night with her, her husband, and their two little girls who I found to be so irritating. At this time I knew what people said about pk's (pastors kid's) I almost found this statement to be true; however, you got to remember at this time I was only 16 and just a kid myself trying to live this grown up life. My husband's parents had gotten into church at this time. I tried so hard to try and fit into this family of his but it was as if they had already put a target on me. His mother was so rude to me, constantly reminding me of who I was or still was in her eyes and it didn't matter what I did; I was not changing her mind. I was not one to take peoples insults lightly and I would become so angry and lash right back at her. His sisters were just like their mother cold and rude and no one was ever as "good" as they were. I just didn't know if I could ever really be a part of this family. My husband would defend me but I just couldn't take it. I turned back to what I knew best, drinking and partying, we started going around our old friends again. Partying on Saturday and church on Sunday's still pretending all was the same; but, it wasn't, I would soon find myself being sucked back in to a selfish life style. I succumbed to having an affair on my husband because sex became my biggest addiction and weapon. Sex was used so much in my life to hurt me that I started hurting other people with it, sadly this time my husband would be my target. Maybe things were not the way I expected them to be. Marriage is hard and at 16 almost impossible without God. As I moved further away from God my husband was my "punching bag" and the only way I knew that I could really hurt someone was the way I had been hurt. That was my action of attack and after the affair he got angry. I understood that anger I really did. I just didn't care, "hurting people hurt people," I wrecked our home, broke things, threw things, and left it a complete mess when I left him to go home to my parents' house. Now at 16 you could add one more thing to my list of life; I was divorced, back home with my parents, and out of church again. It was as if I would always destroy everything I touched, nothing ever worked out for me but I thought that I was strong or brave at the time. I realize, now I was weak, scared, and wounded and those wounds don't heal overnight or without the right care. I tended to pour gasoline on my wounds then strike a match thinking it would heal it.

I quickly fell right back into my old routine and partying every night. I could have cared less at this point about anyone who was in my life. My main objective was to fulfill my selfishness. I was hurting and it pleased me to make sure everyone I come in contact with hurt also. I spent the next few months fighting with my ex-husband almost every day he would beg for me to just come back and try again. I just didn't want to, I had a goal and it wasn't to better myself or be married. Then, one day, just out of nowhere, I found out he was leaving for California to marry a new girl. Part of me was extremely happy and the other part of me thought that I just lost out the only real chance I had to get out of this life style; however, I had managed to throw that in the garbage. I am the one who broke this man and left him with really no choice. I am not sure why out of all the things I had done, this one bothered me. I half way felt really bad for the way I treated this man and for the things I did to him. I know this sounds awful but remember up until this point, I had never felt bad for destroying anyone. Maybe it was the fact that I did learn who Jesus was, that he was more than just a name, or just maybe it was the fact that I had found friends that were godly people and it gave me a different perspective. I wouldn't remember until I started writing this book that sometime during all of the partying that the crazy youth pastor I have talked about had actually come to my rescue a few times. I want to add this here to let you know how a little godly love can penetrate any sin someone has in their life. It may not seem like it in the moment but God is smart. As I was telling her about writing this book she began to share with me that one night she had drove to find me in a fetal position laying in a ditch. As she was telling me this I couldn't believe that I didn't remember any of it. I fear what else I don't remember. Part of me is very glad I don't remember everything because most of it is still so painful. Forgiving myself of some of this has been hard; but, so worth it. I have been able to give more of me to God, family, and friends. This love had to have penetrated my heart to have me feeling bad for the way I treated my ex-husband at the time.

Unknown compassion

In the last few years I had to have been shown the love of Jesus. Who would take the time to come and rescue someone like me from a ditch? Only the love of God can send someone to do that; His compassion had to be with this youth pastor. We may not see in the moment God working on us or for us; however, later down the road His works will be revealed; He never leaves our side. It is amazing to me to look back and see what all He was preparing. I would never understand until He was ready to let me in on the plans. He knew then that all the bad I was choosing He was going to use to for His glory. I am so thankful for all the mercy He has had on my life. *Isaiah 55:8) For my thoughts are not your thoughts, neither are your ways my ways, saith the LORD.*

This verse in Isaiah reminds me that I'm the one who chose to walk those dark back roads, God never intended for me to do things on my own. He even sent me help along the way; I just refused to see it and I even turned it against him most of the time. I remember crying out, "why does my life have to be this way?" In fact, it never had to be that way. God isn't going to make us do it this way or that way; He lets us make our own choices. While we are wandering around on the dark back roads, He sends people to guide us out; but, it is up to us if we follow his guidance.

Not my divorce

Life is about to take a big turn, not only am I turning seventeen, divorced, and spending most of my time doing drugs and drinking again; my step dad and mom are going through a divorce. It just seemed so unreal. My mom moved out and I lived at home with my step dad during this time. I would watch him every night drink until he passed out on the couch or where ever else he may be. Seeing this strong kind hearted man be so broken, I began to realize life wasn't fair and would never get easier. I'm sure at this time that any hope I had of life changing vanished with every night I had to watch him drink away the pain. I wasn't hurt by the divorce or even taken by surprise, I knew it was coming, I was hurt by the fact I had to watch my dad hurt. After 18 years of marriage, my parent's lives would change for both of them drastically. Watching your parents go through a divorce is never easy no matter what age you are. Watching everything change people move out, and seeing their stuff leaving with them; makes kids feel as though they are left choosing a parent or feel bad for spending more time with one and not the other. In my case, my dad never made me feel bad about seeing my mom on the other hand my mom was constantly using me to find out what my dad was doing and trying to turn me against him. It was awful, I felt torn even when none of it was my fault. It was during this time that any relationship I may have had with my mom was shredded. She acted as if she despised me for choosing my step-dad and she would constantly remind me that he was not my biological father. I encourage anyone from a broken home to really be cautious of your children, don't pressure them to choose or use them for information. Remind them every day that it is not their fault and that you would never have them choose a side and that you support them no matter what they feel they need to do. They should not have to pay for your choices because they are dealing with a lot already, don't pile your problems on them you are supposed to be the ones who protect them not the ones who break them down. My mom was not my protector or my supporter; she actually pushed me out of her life for not choosing to be with her. How was I to choose? They were both part of my life. I wanted to stay in the home I had always known. My "step-dad" was the one who had always tried to make an effort; but he was always shot down because of the "step" issue. My mom actually made the choice for me she screamed at me how much she hated me and never wanted to see me again.

Life changing

One more piece of news would come this year. In all of my searching for love, it would finally pay off; just not in the way I expected nor did I ever expect love to be so hard. Again I was hanging out with my old friends and finding myself doing the same old things I had been doing most of my life. I reconnected with the one friend I thought I could have had a life with and we would find ourselves taking off on weekends just to get out of town trying to just escape the reality of life by just going away. We would drive for hours and just sleep in the car or on a lake, just where ever we would find ourselves, we would get lost in long talks. It was like the opportunity we missed was being given a second chance. We would have so much fun, we laughed, we cried, and we talked about all the things we had been through; it was as if we had never been apart. I wanted so bad for those weekends to never end I wanted to just stay far away from reality and the things I faced every day; however, things wouldn't work out because we would never commit to each other so I felt the need to settle for someone very close to my friend. This would soon back fire and not be even close to what I had expected it to be. I was so foolish in my actions.

I became pregnant and my life was threatened and was only given one option, abortion. I had been down this road before and I wouldn't end this life I was carrying. I wasn't happy about being pregnant nor did I really know what would happen but I would step up to the plate. Never did the thought to do anything other than raise my child come to mind as I begin to progress in my pregnancy; however, I was afraid I would not be able to do it alone.

My ex-husband was back in town and going through another divorce that was not pretty. I felt the need to be what I wasn't when we were married. We started talking again and he knew my circumstance and seemed ok with it. I thought I would never find anyone else who would be ok with the choices I had made and the situation I was facing. We decided to remarry and make things work, yes, my ex-husband became my current husband. We made things work, it was hard at times. Not only did I have to deal with what I had done to our marriage but I had given up drugs and alcohol the moment I found out I was pregnant and the withdrawals were very hard. It was an easy choice to rid these things from my life when I knew I wasn't breathing for just me but the struggle of quitting was challenging at times. I made it all almost ten months and I knew I had that battle won I would never touch another drug in my life I told myself.

As I held my beautiful baby boy in my arms I knew for the first time what love really felt like he had to be the most beautiful person I had ever seen. He was perfect, not a single flaw, he was my life changer. He stole my heart the first time he looked in my eyes. Somewhere I got lost again, I don't know if it was the long nights of being a new mom or the stress of a struggling marriage; but, drinking quickly made its way back in my life and I found myself struggling with being a new mom and wife with no place to turn. So I found myself going around some of the same old people, falling back into that darkness, and slowly thinking that there was something better out there; I was so blinded by this horrible life style. I would soon leave my husband and lose my son to my husband and his family. I ended up in jail and with nothing. Jail didn't bother me nor did losing everything I had; but, losing my son that ripped my heart from my chest I would lay awake every night and cry as I set in my jail cell. After getting out of jail I would find myself fighting with my now, once again ex-husband. Every day, all day long, I thought how unfair that I couldn't even hold my baby boy. I remember him using my son against me, for example he would call me and say, "I'll let you see him but you have to meet me at the police department." I would go and set and wait for him to only have him say, "No I changed my mind." I remember the rage I felt over him keeping my son from me I could not believe this was happening. Part of me thought, "Oh how I deserved this for all the things I have done," the other part of me thought, "how unfair this was." He held an advantage over me; he had the one thing I would lay my life down for. The one person I would gladly do anything for. I remember that pain like it was yesterday a pain I never wanted to feel again, it hurt so bad. I didn't think I would be able to make it without my baby. Enough was enough this would be the time I would begin to change everything. From this point it was not only affecting me; it was affecting my son. I would be however or whoever I needed to be, I had to just to get my baby boy back in my arms. If I had to play his cat and mouse game I would do it whatever he wanted me to do or be. I did and it worked, soon my son was back in my arms and I vowed that I would do anything to keep it that way; no matter what the cost would be. Eventually I went back to my ex-husband and we begin to try to work things out and I would soon find out I was pregnant again. We made the decision to move off, out of state, unmarried, just trying to work on things, to start over on a journey together as a family, and we left everything and everyone we knew in hopes that we would be able to be a family. That was the hardest part, even though I thought I was alone, I would really be alone in this new place. I had nothing to fall back on in this new state and nowhere to run. He was battling trusting me; I can't say I didn't blame him because I didn't really trust myself to be honest. Every fight turned into a constant reminder of what I had done I not only would be reminded by everyone who knew me but

I would be reminded by the very man who said he forgave me. I struggled with thinking he would never really be able to forgive me and this made it almost impossible to forgive myself. We would fight constantly and I felt as if I would never be good enough for him. Things would never get any better than what they were and I couldn't pretend myself out of this and grew rather angry at myself. I would take all of this anger I felt out on him and our relationship would become one full of physical abuse from both parties. This would go on for quite some time and we finally decided things had to change. Maybe if I would get a job to get me out of the house, meet new people, and bring in some income; that would help. So six months pregnant I went to work, it was difficult; but, it helped a lot. Maybe the break from one another or the fact we both had new things to talk about. We were able, after a little while, to begin to mend our friendship and really work on things. After our second son was born, we would take a trip home to visit our family and show that things were working out. We decided to remarry on this trip home because we both knew that just living together was not right and we were finally getting along and working things out; so we jumped back into marriage.

Words on Marriage

I would like to add my personal thought's on the marriage issue I found myself dealing with. I can give every excuse possible on why I made the choices I did; however, marriage is meant to be a beautiful thing. You both are meant to encourage and to be a help to one another. In my case I stepped out of my marriage, I committed adultery, and the bible tells us adultery is a sin and even goes as far as to say it is punishable by death. It is one of the biblical reasons for a divorce my husband was given the opportunity to walk away biblically and never look back. When he choose to stay and forgive me, then he closed that door and if we would have been where we should have been with God, there would have been a difference in both of us. He wouldn't have hung that over my head and I wouldn't have kept making the same mistake over and over. We both made mistakes in the way we handled our marriage and the way we tried to fix it.

Let's talk about the story of David a man after God's on heart. He called for a woman who did not belong to him, a woman who was married to one of his men in war. He lay down with this woman and tried to keep it a secret and she became pregnant. David goes as far as to try and get her husband to leave the battle to come home and be with his wife in hopes that he could make the pregnancy appear to be of the husband. The husband refused saying; "He would not leave his men," so David had him sent to the front line so that he would be killed in action. One mistake in David's life led to another man's murder. His sin led him to try and cover up what he did with no success and eventually getting another man killed.

One sin will lead you into so many, one after another. Jesus paid the price for each one of us so that we may be forgiven of our sins. Getting the Lord's forgiveness is one thing because he loves us unconditionally, it is hard for people to forgive people, we think if we forgive then we are giving up the power we hold over them. Forgiveness isn't just for one or the other it is for both parties, the bible says over and over to forgive.

Matthew 18 21) Then came Peter to him, and said, Lord, how oft shall my brother sin against me, and I forgive him? till seven times? 22) Jesus saith unto him, I say not unto thee, Until seven times: but, Until seventy times seven.

Just think about how many times we are forgiven for our sins on a daily basis what if Jesus said never again will I forgive.

To the party who needs to forgive, I know you are hurt and angry. I know you feel like you are giving up that power but what you are really doing is releasing yourself from a prison, by no means will it be easy; but, it will be worth it. You will be able to move on with your life, you will be freed from that hurt or anger that you have. Every situation is different and I would strongly advise you to seek God. I do want you to understand though that there is power in forgiveness. There are many people I have forgiven for the wrongs they done to me and it was in those times I felt I could really breathe again; I wasn't suffocated by the hurt anymore. Forgiving myself was much harder. I still battle with this sometimes. Asking for forgiveness though that was the hardest I hate that I hurt so many people but with my hand in the Lord's, He has helped me through it.

No erasing

I want to take the next few chapters to reflect on all I have told you. I battled feeling out of place which led to a whole lot of struggle and pain. These emotions are real and they can drive a person to places they never thought they would go. They can lead to many addictions that are hard to break, none which can be done alone; but, all can be done with God's help. Thinking back on all the different events that took place in my life it would be easy to feel sorry for myself or even be disgusted with the things I did. Don't get me wrong, I would love to erase a few chapters of my life; however, I also know that these things made me who I am today and these events made me able to be a person who can relate to what other people face and to show people there is hope in Jesus Christ.

It wasn't without a lot of tears and hurt; however, all those roads traveled made me who I am today. A person who can stand tall and know firsthand that nothing is too big for God. I know that God was preparing me for the call He would later place on my life. There is more to my story and I hope to one day share it with everyone. I just want you to know that your past does not have to determine who you are today. You can rip off and throw away any names that have been attached to you. Today you can have a new name in Jesus and you can be a person who God uses; it is never too late.

Youth Pastor

I talked a little about my youth pastor in my life, there are many more details about this woman of God. We had a very rocky relationship to say the least and at times I hated her; yet, sometimes I needed her. She would constantly quote scripture after scripture to me; but, sometimes she would just listen and say "I'm praying for you kid." Those times I would roll my eyes and think, 'What good are you? That really does not help me, all I need is some guidance or someone to agree with me or even tell me I was wrong." Today I can see it was those prayers that helped me make it through all the trials I faced. She was pleading my case to the father and He was answering her prayers. Today I call this woman my mom, my kids call her Nannie, she is also the pastor of our church, and a friend to so many. She has been a shoulder to cry on, a smack of reality when needed, and hand up when I would fall. When I was in her youth group I learned a verse I would quote constantly;

1st Timothy 4: 12) Let no man despise thy youth; but be thou an example of the believers, in word, in conversation, in charity, in spirit, in faith, in purity.

At the time I thought I was being smart, basically telling people you can't look down on me just because I'm young. Later I would find out that Paul wrote this to Timothy to encourage him to keep going forward in God and for Timothy to be that example to all old and young. I had at one point when I was living right preached a message around this verse titled; Hammer or Mirror What Do You Use Your Bible As?

As a youth pastor today this is still one of my favorite verses not because I want my kids to use it against others but because I want them to use it against their own flesh to fight those feelings of; I'm nobody, I'm too young, or I'm never going to make it. God has called who so ever will and age is not a requirement. The requirement is in the second part of the verse. I want them to use it as a guideline of how to live. I believe my youth pastor was my Paul she was to teach and encourage me to go on God's path she was an example in these areas. I look back and smile as I am blown away by how God works, He was teaching me a lesson for my position today all those years ago. We can find in many bible verses that God knows all and plans all. He knows his plans for us and has set them in motion long before we even step up. He is in control of all, He has always and will forever have His hand out just waiting for us to come to him.

Luke 19:10) For the Son of man is come to seek and to save that which was lost.

Ephesians 2:8) For by grace are ye saved through faith; and that not of yourselves: it is the gift of God: 9 Not of works, lest any man should boast .

Jeremiah 29:11) For I know the thoughts that I think toward you, saith the Lord, thoughts of peace, and not of evil, to give you an expected end.

Lesson's learned

I have learned over the years when God intended for us to take the stairs straight up to the top of the mountain, on the path he has prepared for us, we think we know better. We decide we know better and should just walk around to the other side in hopes that it won't be as steep, only to find out the stairs would have been so much easier! I have taken many back roads and know without a doubt I still have lots of traveling to do before getting up the mountain. Even while taking my own way God has provided resting points along the way, He has sheltered me from the storms I have created and, fed me when I was hungry and I know he will continue to do so. Today I don't blame God for anything as a matter of fact I thank him for protecting me while I was making all the wrong choices. He took me from my mess and He's giving me the chance to be a vessel that He can use. Do I still have cleaning up? Yes I do, we all do, we just have to be willing to let him clean do the cleanup. Realizing my biggest addiction was myself and letting him break that addiction has opened my eyes to why I did a lot of the things I did. Self-addiction left me saying things like "I will repay those who hurt me." What I had learned was that you could never depend on anyone, at some point everyone would let you down, and everything was a lie. So I had taught myself to depend only on me. Letting God break that addiction is one of the hardest things to do and I still battle it today because I had never learned to depend on anyone. Thinking that I had to give trust to this "God" I could not see was almost impossible for me. I struggle today even with keeping my faith placed in the Lord even though He can do so much better and more than I ever can. It's hard to believe that it gets easier as He continues to prove to me just how much He can do when I truly put my faith in Him.

How do I put my trust in God? You have to be willing to know and trust He is real and that He is on your side no matter what life throws your way. I remember setting in my chair at church and saying things like, "God if you're real then have them play that song about rolling the stone away." I kept it real vague in case people around me could hear my thoughts, I would know what the song was but I wouldn't say the name and there are many songs about rolling a stone away. Sure enough, the song, would come on next, I would think, "no way!" So I would quickly say something like, "ok fine make the drummer drop his drum stick," sure enough I remember his drum stick fell to the floor. If anyone was looking at me they probably thought I was having a heart attack as my facial expression was that of a deer in headlights!!! Maybe, it was all a coincidence; but, it was enough for me at first to know He was real. Since then, I have felt God and I know without a doubt He is real. I have built that relationship with him that is unlike any other type of relationship you can have.

How can a relationship be made with the Lord? The same way it can with anyone here on earth. I tell my youth group that you can talk to Him the same as you can me. There is no right or wrong ways to talk to the Lord just simply talk to Him and He wants you to. He is the best listener I know, He hears every word even the ones you can't get out. Giving up "self" was one of the best things I have done because I was able to replace me with God and through Him I can do all things as He is my strength. I don't have to worry about every little thing because I know God's got it I know I will be taken care of as long as I live for Him, I will never face another problem alone. He is ready and able to be this kind of friend to every single one of us after all that's why the cross was built that's why there was blood shed on Calvary.

Is it really possible?

Going through all I went through, it is easy to relate to some issues people face. I know that pain that is attached with each one; I have felt that pain, I know the struggle of laying them down and never picking them up again, I know it may seem impossible to get out of the situation you're in and to break the addiction's that may have a hold on your life. The impossible is so very possible with God. He is able to do so much more than you can ever imagine. Not only that, but you don't have to let those things define who you are today or who you will be tomorrow. He is ready to take those defining things in your past or present life and get rid of them. People may still remember and still try to break you down by reminding you; even I battle this today. My mind is made up and I'm moving on. I know that I'm not who I was nor will I ever be that person ever again. God has a plan for me and for you. "Those people" can talk all they want; but, I'm not going to let their words have power over my life any longer. I am taking a stand that God has the truth about who I am not those people.

How do I start this life this change?

Frist we can find in *Romans 10:9 9 That if thou shalt confess with thy mouth the Lord Jesus, and shalt believe in thine heart that God hath raised him from the dead, thou shalt be saved.*

Secondly, we begin to live a life style that is fitting to the Lord we can learn this life style by studying his word. Finding a church to attend and surround ourselves with fellow believers. As we do this we are forming that relationship with the Lord. Make it personal to you, my relationship with the Lord is very much designed just for me. I tell people all the time I teach, preach, and pray different from anyone else I know. Guess what, that is ok. God made each of us unique, no one is the same so the way we do things is also going to be different. The important thing is speak the truth with love. I am so thankful for the life I have been blessed with and I have way more than what I deserve. I'm so thankful for His mercy and love. I'm thankful that Jesus went to the cross so that we would have the opportunity to have eternal life. I could go on forever naming all the things I'm thankful for but I will end with I'm thankful for the new name I have been given.

No longer am I on back roads- lost in sin, but I can walk hand in hand with Jesus and win.

Dear readers,

I wanted to take the opportunity to say thank you I appreciate everyone for your encouragement, your support, and your prayers. I believe without a doubt that this book is to help someone who is or has struggled with some or all of the things I faced. Writing this was also a whole new healing for me I was able to face some of these things head on for the first time in my life and not feel defeated by them. I know that God has a plan for not only me but every one of you.

I pray that the Lord begin to open doors and break down walls, that you are encouraged to step out in faith and do things in the Lord that you have never done. That you wake up with an enjoyment for the life the Lord has given you and that you share his love with others.

In Jesus name Amen.